By Michael Teitelbaum

Illustrated by
Paige Billin-Frye

Random House 🏠 New York

What do zombies serve
at tea?

Lady fingers.

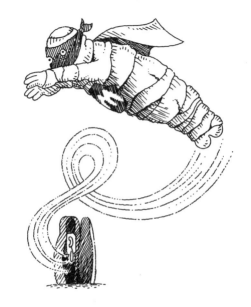

What is the one thing that can harm Super-Mummy?

Crypt-onite.

What do ghosts need
before they can scare
people?

A haunting license.

Why did the Invisible Man forfeit the boxing match?

Because he was a no-show.

Why did the mummy miss
the party?
_____

Because she was all
wrapped up in her work.

Why did the ghoul bury
the trophy?

Because she wanted it engraved.

How did the corpse get
out of the coffin?

It wormed its way free.

What position did the ghost play in the baseball game?

_____

Fright field.

Why was the
archaeologist crying?

Because he wanted his mummy.

What kind of ship does a
vampire sail?

A blood vessel.

What do you call a magic competition among witches?

_____

A spelling bee.

What has fur, howls at the moon, and is easy to clean?

A wash-and-werewolf.

Who do monsters buy
their cookies from?

The Ghoul Scouts.

Why aren't ghosts allowed
in beauty parlors?

Because they're too
hair-raising.

Where do monsters go
swimming?

In Lake Eerie.

What did the ghost's
mother say to her son on
Halloween night?

"You be scareful out there tonight!"

Why couldn't
Frankenstein dance?

Because he had two left feet.

What did the ghouls eat
at the barbecue?

_____

Handburgers and hot dogs.

What do grave robbers
wear in the rain?

Ghoul-oshes.

Who gets rid of ghosts in henhouses?

Eggs-orcists.

How do ghosts fly?

In scareplanes.

Who did the ghoul hire to
write her autobiography?

A ghost writer.

What do you call a skull
with a candle in it?

_____

A headlight.

How does a phantom in
New York talk to a spirit
in California?

They make a
ghost-to-ghost phone call.

What did the monster get
at the beauty parlor?

A new scare-do.

Who did the mummy call
when he got hungry?

Tomb service.

What did the monster's aunt say when she came to visit him?

_____

"You grue-some since I last saw you."

What does a ghost buy at
a health food store?

Supernatural food.

Where do vampires go fishing?

In blood streams.

Where do ghosts go on
Halloween night?

_____

On a shocking spree.

Who makes haunted-
house calls?

Witch doctors.

Why did the black cat
cross the road?

To bring bad luck to the
other side.

What does a witch drink
her coffee out of?

A cup and sorcerer.

What does a Hungarian zombie eat for dinner?

Ghoulash.

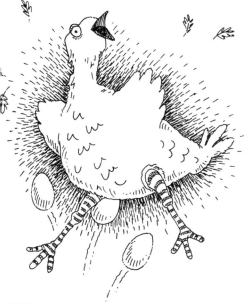

What do you get when you scare a chicken?

Bedeviled eggs.

What did the polite
vampire say when he
didn't want any more to
eat?

"No fangs!"

What do you find in a
haunted hive?

Zom-bees.

Why didn't the corpse
come out to play?

Because he was feeling
rotten.

What kind of spirits live
in hardware stores?

Spirits of turpentine.

Why did the witch pass
out over her cauldron?

Because she'd cast a
fainting spell.

What is a mummy's
favorite kind of music?

Wrap music.

What do you call a
magician in an airplane?

A fly·ing sorcerer.

Where do ghosts go when
they die?

The happy haunting ground.

Why did the cannibal
eat the captain of
the track team?

Because he liked
fast food.

What does a ghoul order
in an ice-cream parlor?

A dead-man's float.

What do you call a
happy-go-lucky ghost?

A scarefree spirit.

Where does Dracula go to work?

The Vampire State
Building.